G³L A²D

7 Principles for a Happier Life

G³L A²D

7 Principles for a Happier Life.

ERIC J. RAFF

ISBN 9781730781841
Published in the United States of America

Book Design by Eric J. Raff
Illustrations adapted by Eric J. Raff

EPIC CONSULTING, LLC
515 East 85th Street, Suite 4F
New York, NY 10028

To my uncle,
Captain Edward Dangler, USN (Ret.),
my role model for how to live a life of purpose,
integrity, ongoing learning, and happiness.

CONTENTS

INTRODUCTION

Congratulations—you've just taken the first step to a happier life!

Whether you're happy most of the time, not so happy and searching for greater joy in life, or are somewhere in between and looking for something that will bring you greater joy, satisfaction, and happiness, I will promise you this: if you're willing to follow the principles presented in *GLAD*, and will take the time to do some (if not all) of the exercises at the end of each section, you will be a happier person and have better tools to deal with the ups and downs of life after reading *GLAD* than you had before.

Are You Happy?

Last year, the self-improvement industry in the United States was estimated at $11 billion dollars and is expected to keep growing. And with good reason. Research studies show that happy people are liked more by others, are more productive in their jobs, are more likely to get married and stay married, benefit from lower levels of stress, lower blood pressure, reduced neuroendocrine, inflammatory, and cardiovascular activity, and have stronger romantic and social relationships than people who are less happy. *Wow*—all that just from being happy? No wonder the self-improvement industry is worth billions of dollars!

Short-term Happiness Tips

A number of helpful recommendations have come out of the many empirical studies done in the field of happiness, the findings from which are not only interesting and enlightening but have been shown to increase people's happiness if they follow them. For example, research studies have shown that people can lift their happiness in the short-term by doing any of the following:

- Listen to upbeat music (My 'happy' music is Latin or Reggae.)

- Exercise or go for a "happy" walk—a "happy" walk is acting as if you're happy when walking. (We'll talk more about *"acting as if"* later.)

- Smile more often, practice optimism, and do more fun things that bring laughter and joy into your life.

- Choose colors artfully as colors have been shown to have different effects on our moods. (Did you know that a blue sky can make you feel more peaceful or that green inspires calmness, comfort, and happiness?)

- Surround yourself with scents or smells that have a positive effect on your mood. (Citrus scents re-energize and re-invigorate moods.)

- Avoid comparing yourself to others, be grateful for what you have, and reframe your attitude from thinking about what you don't have to being appreciative for what you *do* have. (Expressing gratitude is a key element of happiness, and we'll talk about this later as well.)

- Do a good deed, or do more than one while you're at it, or volunteer to help others. (Research shows that helping others makes *you* happy.)

- Practice Meditation and do Yoga (Even if you can't sit still for more than a few minutes at a time or don't think you can stretch like the person in front of you, the benefits from meditation and Yoga have been shown to be significant.)

- Get a good night's sleep (try for at least seven hours a night). People who don't get enough rest are more sensitive to negative emotions, which can affect their levels of happiness.

- Get a pet if you don't have one or take care of a plant. (I had a small *Betta* fish that made me happier than I would have thought possible and bought some plants that I like watering and watching grow.)

- Live in the present moment and *decide* you're going to be happier. (Research has shown that positive intentions can work wonders.)

- Build good friendships, get married, and maintain positive life-long relationships with people you like (or love) and who feel the same way about you. (Positive relationships and strong social connections are a key factor in people's ongoing happiness.)

With all the research that's been done on happiness and all the empirical results from these studies that have been shared in books, articles, and online, you'd think most people living in the U.S. would be pretty happy, right? Wrong. In the *United Nations World Happiness Report 2018,* America ranked 18th out of 156 countries surveyed. And according to a 2017 Harris Poll Survey of American

Happiness, only 33 percent of Americans surveyed said they were happy.

So, I have a question for you: are you part of the happy 33% or part of the unhappy 67%? Here's another question: If you identify more with the folks in the *un*happy group, then why is that? If the secrets to being happier can be found in all of those books, tapes, webinars, seminars, and research studies, then why are so many people not as happy as they'd like to be? Isn't anyone reading the literature on happiness other than the researchers doing the studies? Or are people reading these books and research findings and just not following the recommendations?

One explanation could be due to what researchers call the *set-point theory of happiness,* which says that about 50% of our happiness is determined by our *genes*—heredity and personality traits that stay constant throughout our

15

lives and which for the most part isn't under our control. *Circumstances,* which most people incorrectly think are directly responsible for how happy we feel, and which we usually blame for our unhappiness when things don't go our way, only account for about *10%* of our happiness (unless they're really dismal, in which case they have a greater impact on our happiness). *You may be thinking: how is that possible—whether we're rich or poor, healthy or unhealthy, happy with where we live, or what we look like, our circumstances only increase our happiness for a short time and only by a mere 10 percent?*

Yep, and it's because of something researchers call *hedonic adaptation,* which says that people adapt pretty quickly to

> An object in possession seldom retains the same charm that it had in pursuit.
> —*Pliny the Younger*

16

circumstantial changes in their life—they may make you happier for a while, but your happiness is unlikely to last long.

If that's hard to believe, think about a time in your life when your circumstances changed for the better—maybe you got a raise at work, moved to a new and nicer location, got married, or landed a new job. Any of these changes probably made you happier when they first happened, but over time you got used to them and they stopped giving you the same boost of happiness as when they first happened. Sooner or later you adapted to the change and started looking around for other things that would make you happy.

Does that surprise you? If so, it might surprise you even more to know that your *thoughts, actions, and attitudes* are responsible for about *40%* of your level of happiness— almost half of how happy you feel! This is so important it's worth repeating: *thoughts, actions, and attitudes* have a bigger impact on how happy we feel than our circumstances do.

Changing our behaviors—which is more under our control than changing our genes or our circumstances, will have a bigger impact on our level of well-being and happiness than anything else we can do. The net takeaway? Our happiness isn't somewhere "out there" waiting for us. It's within us, and the key to unlocking it—*our thoughts, actions, and attitudes,* is in our hands.

So, my answer to the question I asked earlier: *why are so many people not as happy as they'd like to be,* is twofold: The first is that many people just aren't willing to put in the effort to do what research says will make them happier—and it does take effort. The second, and more important reason, I think, is that most of the literature on happiness offers *short-term* happiness fixes, or individual and *unconnected* behavior changes, instead of recommending a *comprehensive and unified* approach to living a more meaningful, enjoyable, and integrated life over the *long-term.*

I'm not saying you shouldn't have fun or pursue short-term happiness-building activities whenever you can. On the contrary—life is made up of many more small, happy moments than large ones and you should build as many pleasurable, fun, exciting, and joyful moments into your life as possible since happy moments are cumulative, give us joy when we think back on them, and add up to a happy life. What I *am* saying, is that short-term fun activities, as enjoyable as they are, will only keep you happy for so long *(hedonic adaptation)* and unless they're connected to a bigger, more personal and meaningful endgame, may not satisfy your goal of long-term, sustainable happiness.

Sure, there are lots of useful suggestions and helpful advice that can be found in the many books and articles written on happiness, but personally, I didn't find what I was looking for—a long-term, sustainable approach to living an integrated and meaningful life based on what research says are the key principles of happiness.

Which is why I wrote GLAD.

7 Core Principles

After researching self-help books, articles, and studies on happiness, I consolidated into seven core principles what I believe are the keys to living a happier, more satisfying life. I then grouped these principles into a short, simple, and easy-to-remember formula that I call *GLAD*—or more accurately, *G^{3}LA^{2}D*, since the formula is made up of three "G's": *Goals, Gratitude,* and *Good karma*; one "L": *Let it go*; two "A's": *Attitude* and *Act as if*; and one "D": *Do it.*

The Research Isn't New—the Approach Is

There are three points I'd like to make to any potential reader of *GLAD*. The first is that no new research in the field of happiness was conducted by me in the writing of *GLAD*. Each of the principles outlined in this book is based on research findings presented in scholarly books, research journals, and articles published on happiness by well-known researchers and psychologists in the areas of happiness and positive psychology, the field of study that focuses on well-being and optimal health (e.g., what makes life worth living), instead of on dysfunction and unhealthy behaviors.

Some readers will be familiar with the research that *GLAD* is based on, while others may be learning it for the first time. Either way, the *GLAD* method for living a more fulfilling and happier life will be new to all readers. And while each of the core principles is *individually* important and will bring greater happiness into your life on their own, you'll maximize the value of GLAD when you build as many of the principles into your life as you can. As the saying goes, *the whole is greater than the sum of its parts.* As you'll soon see, each principle in *GLAD* is connected to, supports, and impacts each other—and when taken together, will have a powerful effect on the quality of your life and your *long-term* happiness.

The second point is that *GLAD* is not meant to be a comprehensive summary of all the research findings reported in the field of happiness and positive psychology. The content is based on research findings that resonated with me. My goal in writing *GLAD* is to present the approach I came up with in short, easy-to-read, and easily under-standable chapters so that readers can build these key happiness principles into their life without having to read as many books in the field of happiness or positive psychology as I did—unless they want to. Any reader interested in more detailed or more in-depth information on any of the topics presented in *GLAD* is encouraged to check out the books and articles listed in the bibliography.

The third and final point is that the *GLAD* formula is not a substitute for therapy. While I sincerely believe that the principles in *GLAD* can significantly improve the quality of your life and your long-term level of happiness, there are times in each of our lives when no amount of self-help or research findings can effectively address certain issues we may be facing. When you're dealing with serious life issues, or when your personal life history or circumstances become overwhelming or more than you can handle on your own, a professional therapist is often the best solution to provide the guidance and support you need to help you cope most effectively.

But for those other times, for the majority of the issues we each have to deal with as we go about our day-to-day lives, it's important to have an approach or philosophy that will help guide our thinking, behaviors, and actions. The approach that's been most useful for me is to think through the seven core principles outlined in *GLAD*.

Whenever I'm not sure what action to take or how I should approach an issue I may be wrestling with, I review each principle to see which one applies best to the situation I'm facing. Building the G^3LA^2D formula into my life has led to a much greater sense of purpose, guidance, and happiness for me and I'm confident it will do the same for you!

EVOLVE LIKE A FROG

W hy illustrate a book on happiness with frogs? Simple. The humble frog is much more than a likeable little amphibian: it's a symbol of rebirth, regeneration, and transformation and represents pretty much what *GLAD* is all about—an approach to living and positive growth that can transform and change your life for the better and bring increased levels of happiness to all areas of your life.

And the seven principles in *GLAD* will do just that—help you evolve and change for the better, just like nature's friend, the frog, which transitions in its life journey from tadpole to adult status when it reaches its full potential.

The frog's connection to water is also symbolic of cleansing as we wash out negativity and bad energy, adapt to ongoing changes in our global and personal environments and navigate the currents of our own transitions as we continue to grow and evolve along our own life journeys.

It should be pointed out however, that while the frog illustrations are light-hearted and fun, the process of change and transition for many people can be a challenging and serious road to navigate.

So, as you read through *GLAD* and reflect on the content and different exercises in each chapter, remember the little frog and how it evolves and adapts across the course of its life. Like the frog, we're all capable of adapting and transitioning to whatever changes or opportunities may come our way, and when we do, we'll experience a more fulfilling, enjoyable, and happier life.

If you're ready to explore how the *G^{3}LA^{2}D* principles can help you live a more purposeful, compassionate, satisfying, and happy life, then turn the page and let's begin with the first of the three "G's": *GOALS.*

G^{3}LA^{2}D: 7 PRINCIPLES FOR A HAPPIER LIFE

GOALS

G^{3}LA^{2}D: 7 PRINCIPLES FOR A HAPPIER LIFE

> My goal is simple.
> It is a complete understanding
> of the universe, why it is
> as it is and why it
> exists at all.
> —*Stephen Hawking*

S tephen Hawking was one of the greatest minds of our time and one of the most respected and well-known theoretical physicists since Einstein. And despite being struck down at age twenty-one with motor neuron disease (better known as *"Lou Gehrig's disease"*), which left him almost completely paralyzed, he became one of the most well-recognized scientists who ever lived, a best-selling author, was married twice, and had three children. But as impressive as that is, what I found even more inspiring than his intellectual accomplishments, was his incredible attitude and sense of life. Hawking was quoted as saying, *"I don't have much positive to say about motor neuron disease, but it taught me not to pity myself because others were worse off, and to get on with what I could still do. I'm happier now than before I developed the condition."*

Amazing, right? After losing nearly all of his motor skills and his ability to communicate without a speech-generating device, he was still able to accomplish everything he did and find happiness in his life, while many of us with good physical health and so many other positive things going for us, gripe about the smallest inconveniences and constantly complain when we're not happy. Which begs the question: what in the world did Hawking have (other than an extraordinarily brilliant mind) that's in our power to have, but that we haven't yet found?

Happiness researchers might answer that Hawking's amazing ability to experience happiness despite his life-changing disability can be explained by *hedonic adaptation*, the idea that positive and negative changes in our life situation only make us happier or sadder for a short period of time before we eventually return to our baseline, or *"set point"* of happiness.

Critics of hedonic adaptation however, think the theory is too general and doesn't take the individual or their unique circumstances into account. In the case of a traumatic illness like Stephen Hawking's, I agree with the critics and offer an explanation other than hedonic adaptation to explain Hawking's remarkable ability to transcend his challenging life situation. The explanation can be found in his quote at the beginning of this chapter. Hawking had a *Goal*—a well-defined, consistent, and personally motivating goal that gave him purpose, meaning, and a sense of control over his life. And not just any goal—his goal was to obtain *a complete understanding of the universe, why it is as it is and why it exists at all.* That's one extraordinary goal.

> Happiness is the progressive realization
> of a worthy ideal, or goal.
>
> — *Earl Nightingale*

It's probably safe to say that most of us won't have a goal as audacious as Stephen Hawking's. But without personally meaningful goals to give our lives a sense of purpose, many people will continue to feel that there's something missing in their lives—something, that if they only knew what it was, would give them the fulfillment they've been longing for to make them *happy.* To "fill" the hole in their lives many people run from one fun activity to another or buy new clothes or "toys" that they hope will give their lives the meaning and satisfaction they've been missing. But at the end of the day, the hole remains unfilled.

No doubt you've heard the saying, "Happiness is a journey." As clichéd and comforting as that is, I believe the message is backwards. Happiness isn't a journey—the *journey* is happiness. The process of choosing and pursuing goals that are important to you and that are connected to a broader purpose in your life—not collecting *things*, is what brings us joy, fulfillment, and happiness.

Viktor Frankl, author of *Man's Search for Meaning,* which recounted his experiences as an Auschwitz concentration camp inmate during World War II, wrote that our primary drive in life is not pleasure as Sigmund Freud believed, but the discovery and pursuit of what we *personally find meaningful*—in other words, having clear and consistent goals.

A favorite quote of Frankl's was from Friedrich Nietzsche, the famous German philosopher, who wrote, *"He who has a why to live for can bear almost any how."* According to Frankl, *"The greatest need of human beings is for a sense of meaning and purpose in life, for a goal to work toward."*

Our culture expects and demands happiness, yet Frankl didn't think it was something we should seek directly. He defined happiness as a *by-product* of forgetting ourselves in a task which draws on our imagination and talents. The Japanese even have a word for it—*IKIGAI* (pronounced *ee-kee-guy*), which is most closely translated as *"a reason for being."* Your Ikigai is your motivation for getting up in the morning. It's your reason to enjoy life and is similar to the French phrase "raison d'être," which means *reason to be*, or, *purpose.*

In Japanese culture it's widely thought that everyone has an Ikigai—a purpose in life, a reason to get out of bed. It's

36

about finding out what keeps you motivated and makes you happy. But more than that, it looks to answer the question, *what should I do with my life?* That's not an easy question for most of us to answer, but when you do, when you figure out what makes you jump out of bed in the morning, your health and happiness increase. And not only will your health and happiness improve, but according to Dan Buettner and Ed Diener, authors of *The Blue Zones of Happiness: Lessons from the World's Happiest People, "Research has shown that knowing your sense of purpose is worth up to seven years of extra life expectancy."* In the span of an average life, that's a pretty good increase!

The purpose or *why* for Hawking was to have a complete understanding of the universe. The goal or goals you choose to pursue should be whatever will give a sense of purpose and direction to YOUR life—something that is personally meaningful and motivating to you.

We should concern ourselves
not so much with the pursuit of happiness,
but with the happiness of pursuit.

—Hector and the Search for Happiness

Viktor Frankl's definition of happiness is similar to the concept of flow—a mental state that's come to be known as "being in the zone." Flow was named by Mihaly Csikszentmihaly, a psychologist who found that "happiness is not something that happens." According to Csikszentmihaly, we experience flow (enjoyment and happiness) when our skills and the challenges we apply them to intersect. If a task is too easy for our skills, we become bored. If a task is too difficult for our skills we worry or become anxious. But when the task and our skills are motivating and sufficiently challenging to fully involve and engage us in an activity, we enjoy the task, lose ourselves in it, and experience flow.

WOW! Does that mean our search for how to become happier is over? That all we have to do is lose ourselves in different flow activities that motivate and completely engage us? Well... not quite. I hate to break it to you, but it's not that easy. According to Csikszentmihaly, *"As long as enjoyment follows piecemeal from activities not linked to one another in a meaningful way, one is still vulnerable to the vagaries of chaos."* And chaos isn't what we're after—*a happier life is.* What Csikszentmihaly is saying is that we should choose goals that are not only *individually* important to us, but that are connected to each other, and that over time, will help us achieve whatever ultimate goal we've decided will bring meaning and purpose to our life.

Here's another way to think about it: imagine your life as a jigsaw puzzle and that the different goals you choose to work on throughout your life are interconnecting pieces that all fit together. When each of the individual pieces (sub-goals) are in place, the final picture of your life will be realized and your ultimate goal will be achieved.

The following quote from Csikszentmihaly explains perfectly why the first "G" in the *GLAD* formula is *GOALS* and why it's the foundation for each of the other *GLAD* principles: *"If a person sets out to achieve a difficult enough goal, from which all other goals logically follow, and if he or she invests all energy in developing skills to reach that goal, then actions and feelings will be in harmony, and the separate parts of life will fit together—and each activity will "make sense" in the present, as well as in view of the past and of the future. In such a way, it is possible to give meaning to one's entire life."*

In other words, the journey *is* happiness and choosing a personally challenging goal or sub-group of connected goals that give our life meaning and direction, will motivate and guide us along the journey.

It's not the having, it's the getting.

—*Elizabeth Taylor*

Once you've decided on your goal, your *why*, your reason for being—whether it's creating or pursuing a life's work, doing volunteer or nonprofit work for something you care passionately about, or are committed to learning new knowledge, skills, or experiences to make yourself a better or more informed person—your life will take a new course and you'll have greater levels of happiness than you had before.

When you work toward goals that are personally important to you, are intrinsically motivating, and are connected toward the accomplishment of a larger purpose, you'll be focused, energized, and excited and your life will have structure, direction, and meaning. And you'll be a happier person for it.

But as the saying goes, *"You can't hit a target you're not aiming at."* So, what's your target? What are you aiming at? Where do you want to find yourself one year, five years, ten or twenty years from now? What will make you feel that your life has meaning and importance—something that will be enduring and connect your past to your present and to your future?

Deciding which goals are right for you depends on your values, which define who you are, what you believe in, and what is most important to you in life. Whatever goals you choose for yourself, they should be *authentic*, which means they should reflect *your* values not someone else's. Your goals should support who you are at your core and *fit* you; they should be consistent with your interests and values and match your unique personality.

If you're not sure what goals to pursue it's possible that you don't have clarity on what you really value or which of your values are most important to you. So, let's start with values. What exactly are they?

Values are what give meaning and purpose to your life— they are those things you want to have, hold on to, or pursue, because they enhance your life and are personally relevant and significant to you. And because you want to gain and keep the things you value, they guide the choices and actions you make and ultimately give your life purpose.

Whatever values you want in your life, from the simplest pleasures like a good meal or exercising to stay healthy, to more complex values such as what to do for a living or who to marry, you need to know which of your values are most important to you, *and why*, so that you can make rational decisions about which to pursue, how to prioritize them, and how to integrate them throughout your life.

Happy people typically have goals and values that are well-aligned and integrated. For example, if staying healthy is an important value to you, your goals might include buying organic or unprocessed foods and eating a balance of salads, vegetables, nuts, and fruit. A complementary goal could be to exercise on an ongoing basis, while another supporting goal could include activities like meditation and stress management to support a healthy mental outlook.

If you don't have a good sense of what you value most in your life or aren't sure which potential interests to pursue, then you need to stop thinking about what *might* interest you and *take action* by exploring your different interests to learn which ones excite you. *Thinking* about what you like is fine up to a point, but it's almost impossible to know whether you'll really like doing something until you actually do it.

And it doesn't have to be one thing—there may be lots of things you love and want to pursue, and when they're connected, fully engage you, and give a sense of direction to your life, you'll have found a purpose and meaningful goals to work towards. To recap: figure out what you value in the different areas of your life (e.g. personal, family, career, financial), then develop goals that will help you achieve, keep, and enjoy those values in your life.

An in-depth discussion of values and goal setting is beyond the scope of *GLAD*, but there are many books, articles, and online resources that can help you prioritize your values, set goals that are aligned with them, and guide you through different methods and techniques to help you accomplish the goals you set for yourself.

To help you get started, I've listed some thought-provoking questions and key steps in the goal-setting process below. Additional resources that you can explore on your own are listed in the back of *GLAD*.

IDENTIFYING YOUR VALUES AND GOALS

To get what you want in life you need to prioritize your values and align your goals with them. But before you can set goals, you need to know what you want. The following questions can help you figure that out.

1. What makes your life worth living? When do you feel your happiest? What interests and activities (things that you *value*) make you feel this way?

2. Write down as many things as you can that make your life enjoyable and worthwhile in four key areas of your life (personal, family, career, financial). Now rank them into one of four boxes:

small values, large values, short-term values and long-term values. Now create a values hierarchy for each area of your life by prioritizing the values in each of the four boxes. Next, develop and align your goals with the values you've identified and prioritized.

3. What's missing in your life that if it were filled, would make you happier? Think about what that need *really* represents—keep drilling down until you get to the heart of what you *really need*. For example, you may think you want a promotion for the pay increase you would get, when what you really want is the *recognition* the promotion would bring. If recognition is what you really want and not the additional stress and longer hours the promotion would bring, how else could you get it?

4. What have you accomplished in your life up until now that's given you your greatest sense of happiness and satisfaction?

5. What are you good at that you're also passionate about? If you could do only one thing with your life right now, what would you do?

6. How could you make a living doing it *or* make it a hobby or avocation that gives you more joy and happiness? How could you stop thinking or fantasizing about it and really do it?

7. What price, in terms of time, money or other resources are you willing to give up to achieve what is most important to you?

8. On a scale of 1 – 10, how motivated are you to change your life to increase your happiness?

9. What *one action* could you take now that would move you closer to what you want in your life? What's keeping you from doing it or at least *trying* to do it?

10. Write your obituary—at the end of your life, how will you want your obituary to read?

STEPS TO ACHIEVE YOUR GOALS

If you did some soul-searching and gave serious thought to the questions above, you should have a pretty good idea about what you value and which of your values will bring more meaning and purpose into your life. Below are steps to help you develop and reach your goals.

1. List your most important life goals. Narrow your list to your top three. Select the one that would make

the greatest impact on your life moving forward. This is your key goal, the priority goal each of your other goals should support.

2. List whatever obstacles might come between you and your key goal. Consider what knowledge you might need to acquire, what skills you may need to learn, or whom you may need to contact or network with, to help you remove or work around those obstacles.

3. Create an action plan that lists each step you'll need to take to reach your key goal. Prioritize the action steps you'll need to work on first, second, third, etc.

4. Pick a date to start working on the first step in your action plan. Commit to an expected and realistic completion date.

5. Set benchmarks to track your progress. Course correct as needed as you work on your action plan and tackle each step you've identified.

6. Share your goal with a trusted friend, colleague, or mentor and ask them to keep you focused and on track until you've reached your goal.

Vince Lombardi, the famous NFL coach said, *"Success demands singleness of purpose."* He was right. Don't stretch your time or resources by working on more than one major goal at a time. Stay focused on your key goal until its reached or until it's no longer your key goal. To quote a Russian proverb: *If you chase two rabbits, you will not catch either one.*

Coming up with answers to the above questions may be easier for some people than others. But once you figure out what's really important to you and how to go about making it a reality, you'll have a reason to get out of bed in the morning—you'll have found your *Ikigai* and your purpose. And it doesn't really matter if it's a monumental purpose like Stephen Hawking's, or a more modest purpose that meets *your* needs. If it's important to you and gives you an ongoing sense of direction in your life, you'll experience joy and happiness as you work towards its achievement.

Now that we've covered how important it is to align your goals with values that are personally meaningful and important to you, it's time to explore the other *GLAD* principles for living a well-rounded, more satisfying, and happier life. Let's move on to the next "G": *GRATITUDE.*

GRATITUDE

G^{3}LA^{2}D: 7 PRINCIPLES FOR A HAPPIER LIFE

> If the only prayer you said
> in your life was "Thank you,"
> that would suffice.
>
> —*Meister Eckhart, German*
> *Theologian and Philosopher*

THANK YOU. Two simple words. But don't let their simplicity fool you—the powerful impact these two words can have on your physical and emotional health is extraordinary. According to Sheela Raja, Clinical Psychologist and author of *Overcoming Trauma and PTSD,* "Research suggests that individuals who are grateful in their daily lives actually report fewer stress-related health symptoms, including headaches, gastrointestinal (stomach) issues, chest pain, muscle aches, and appetite problems."

Independent researchers in both England and Hofstra University reported that students who practiced gratitude experienced less stress and depression, received more social support, and were more optimistic and satisfied than those who didn't count their blessings.

Another team of researchers at Indiana University found that cultivating gratitude not only re-wires our brains to make it easier to see the positive things in life, but that the more practice we give our brains at feeling and expressing gratitude, the more we adapt to that mindset. In other words, counting your blessings now makes it easier to notice and count them later. The net result? *The more good you recognize and acknowledge in your life, the happier and more successful you're likely to be.*

Shawn Achor, an American happiness researcher and positive psychology author says, "Something as simple as writing down three things you're grateful for every day for

21 days in a row significantly increases your level of optimism, and it holds for the next six months. The research is amazing." What's also amazing is that studies on happiness found that *gratitude* is the one behavior that tops the list of most impactful happiness skills.

And if findings from current day researchers aren't enough to convince you that gratitude can have a huge impact on your life, then maybe Marcus Aurelius, the famous Roman emperor and philosopher who lived almost two thousand years ago, can convince you. He wrote: *When you arise in the morning, think of what a precious privilege it is to be alive — to breathe, to think, to enjoy and to love.* It certainly seems that the power of gratitude has stood the test of time.

But what if you just don't feel grateful—then what? Not to worry—evidence from studies on gratitude found that we can raise our level of happiness by actively choosing to practice gratitude *even if we don't feel grateful.* That's worth repeating: Even if you don't feel grateful you just need to act as if you're grateful. Btw, *"Act as if"* is one of the two "A's" in our *GLAD* formula, which we'll discuss later. For now, just know that being grateful, or acting as if you're grateful, stimulates the hypothalamus (the part of the brain that regulates stress) and the ventral tegmental area (the part of our "reward circuitry" that's responsible for the sensation of pleasure.)

Which begs the question: what do you have to be grateful about? Well for one thing, how about that you're alive? That fact alone is pretty mind boggling. Dr. Ali Binazir, self-proclaimed Happiness Engineer and author of *"Tao of Dating,"* estimated the probability of being born as 1 in $10^{2,685,000}$ (that's 10 with over two million zeros behind it). I was never good at statistics but learned enough to know the odds were stacked against my being here.

According to Binazir: *Imagine there was one life preserver thrown somewhere in some ocean, with exactly one turtle in all of these oceans, swimming underwater somewhere. The probability that you came about is the same as that turtle sticking its head out of the water — into the middle of that life preserver. On one try.* That's one lucky turtle.

Even if Benazir's probability of being born, or his metaphor about the turtle sticking its head into the middle of a life preserver in the middle of the ocean isn't accurate, a sign that I recently saw at a street fair says pretty much the same thing for people like me who aren't that great at math: *If you are here, you are awesome.*

I definitely agree. The probability that we were born at all, whatever that probability may be, is incredibly small and is as close to experiencing a real-life miracle as you can get.

Which leads one to assume that if you're happy to be alive, you should also be very grateful that you are.

> There are only two ways to live your life.
> One is as though nothing is a miracle.
> The other is as if everything is.
>
> —*Albert Einstein*

So, just what does feeling grateful mean? According to Paula Langguth Ryan, author of *Giving Thanks, The Art of Tithing:*

"Feeling grateful is a sense of what I would call appreciation, wonder, and thankfulness for what has occurred in our lives and what is going on right now, an eager anticipation of what is to come… it's being present to the wonders and joys of life as it is, without wanting it to be different, and a sense of fulfillment that comes from within,

from seeing the good—or the potential for good—in every situation."

But what if, aside from the miracle of your being alive, there's not a whole lot going on in your life for you to be grateful about? How could you go about increasing your sense of gratitude? Here are four suggestions you should seriously consider:

1. RE-FRAME YOUR ATTITUDE

Appreciate what you have and try flipping the negatives you may be focused on to positives. For instance, let's say you were looking forward to a weekend away, but an important client just called with a last-minute project that's due on Monday. You could gripe about how unfair and incon-siderate your client is or you could see it as a chance to step up to the plate and show your value, which could lead to a promotion or end-of-year bonus. If flipping the negatives to positives doesn't work, then try seeing the negatives as learning opportunities that have come your way to help you continue to grow and evolve.

2. PRACTICE MEDITATION, YOGA, OR PRAYER

Each day before you get out of bed express gratitude for another day of life and the possibilities the new day brings. Make time to meditate, do yoga, or say a prayer, if you're religiously or spiritually inclined. Pay attention to the small things in your life that give you pleasure and help you see the beauty that's all around you.

3. DO SOMETHING FOR SOMEONE ELSE

Research shows that helping other people has a positive impact on your own life. So, go do something nice for someone or volunteer your time to a cause that's meaningful to you. If you're not sure what volunteer opportunities to consider, check out www.volunteermatch.org.

4. KEEP A GRATITUDE JOURNAL

Sonja Lyubomirsky, the well-known positive psychologist and author of The How of Happiness, A New Approach to Getting the Life You Want, showed through her research studies that on average people who counted their blessings once a week had a lift in their levels of happiness compared to a control group of people who weren't asked to keep a gratitude journal.

If you'd like to see for yourself if keeping a gratitude journal would have any impact on your happiness, start writing down from three to five things you were grateful for that week. Do it once a week starting on Sunday night and keep it up for the next eight weeks. If you're like the people who participated in the research studies done by Dr. Lyubomirsky, you'll soon start feeling more optimistic and more satisfied with your life. You might even start to feel healthier! And on those days when things are more challenging than usual, looking over your gratitude journal will lift you up, give you hope, and help you see your way through the tougher times of life.

1. I'm grateful for…

   _____

2. I have an appreciation for…

   _____

3. I'm fortunate that…

   _____

4. I feel a sense of wonder when…

   _____

5. I'm very happy that…

   _____

Being grateful doesn't mean that everything in your life is perfect—it means appreciating what's right in your life instead of focusing on what's wrong. There's no doubt that bad things can happen to everyone at one time or another— you get laid off from work, you break up or get broken up with by someone you love, you put on more weight than you ever thought was humanly possible, your kids get in trouble, you don't have kids but can't meet anyone to have them with, a loved one is sick or passed away... or God knows what else may have gone wrong or might go wrong to ruin your day, month, or year. But here's the thing—no matter what challenges you may be facing, there are things in your life you can be grateful for that can help put the other things in perspective. The miracle and beauty of life is all around you—from the sublime to the mundane, but you have to be open to seeing it.

Need a few examples? How about these: the beauty of a summer sunrise or sunset, the amazing colors of trees, flowers, and plants in

> Enjoy the little things in life, for someday you'll realize they were the big things.
> —*Anonymous*

nature, the incredible variety of animal, plant, and insect life on this planet, the changing seasons, the warmth of the sun, the blue of the sky, the gorgeous shapes of clouds and soft breezes at the ocean, the love of your family and friends, a nice and safe place to live, good health and a good job, a smile from a stranger, the lick of a puppy, the smell of fresh brewed coffee or a first sip of wine, the ability to travel and dine at nice restaurants, the miraculous functioning of your body, and countless other things we take for granted every day as we rush through our busy lives. *WHEW!*

And that's just a small sample of all the amazing things in life for which we could be grateful. By training your brain to see the beauty that exists in and all around you, you'll develop an optimistic view of the world and attract more positive energy into your life.

I hope you agree there's a whole lot to be grateful for, and the sooner you start appreciating all the good things you've had, currently have, or will have in the future, the sooner you'll bring greater happiness and positive things or people into your life.

TO DO

1. COUNT YOUR BLESSINGS

   Spend time in quiet introspection and think about what has happened in your life up until now that you are grateful for.

2. KEEP A THREE-SENTENCE HAPPINESS JOURNAL

   Record three positive moments in your day

that are worth remembering. Read it on

days when you need an extra boost!

3. FOCUS LESS ON WHAT YOU WANT

   There will always be things you want.

   Try to focus less on what you want and

   more on what you already have.

4. LIKE YOURSELF

   List three things you like most about yourself

   and why. Remind yourself of these positive

   attributes whenever you need a positive lift.

5. LOOK AT YOURSELF IN THE MIRROR when you

   step out of the shower and marvel at the unique

   miracle that you truly are—*exactly as you are.*

As the Stoic philosopher Epictetus wrote almost two thousand years ago, *"He is a man of sense who does not grieve for what he has not, but rejoices in what he has."*

G^{3}LA^{2}D: 7 PRINCIPLES FOR A HAPPIER LIFE

GOOD KARMA

G^{3}LA^{2}D: 7 PRINCIPLES FOR A HAPPIER LIFE

> What you do makes a
> difference, and you have
> to decide what kind of
> difference you want to make.
>
> —*Jane Goodall*

The third "G" in *GLAD* stands for "Good Karma," which when you think about it, makes good sense following *Gratitude*, since acts of good karma—the kind of karma you want in your life, are often motivated by feelings of gratitude for the good things you have in life. After all, why wouldn't you want to do kind and helpful things for others when you're feeling grateful for all of the good things you have?

Whether you believe in karma or not, I think you'll agree that feeling or not feeling grateful for what you have can positively or negatively influence your thoughts, behaviors, and actions. And when feelings of gratitude lead to positive actions they can set the stage for the recipients of your kindness to also feel gratitude, which may result in their *"paying it forward,"* which creates more positive outcomes—*good karma,* if you will, for everyone!

But what exactly is karma and how can good karma help us have a happy life? *The Free Dictionary* defines karma as follows:

karma

noun kar·ma \ ˈkär-mə also ˈkər- mə \

1. (in Hinduism and Buddhism) action seen as bringing up on oneself inevitable results, in either this life or in a reincarnation.

2. (in Theosophy) the cosmic principle of rewards and punishments for the acts performed in a previous incarnation.

3. the good or bad emanations felt to be generated by someone or something.

A (partial) definition from the *Simple English Wikipedia* states that:

Karma is a word meaning the result of a person's actions as well as the actions themselves. It is a term about the cycle of cause and effect. According to the theory of karma, what happens to a person, happens because they caused it with their actions. It is an important part of many religions such as Hinduism and Buddhism . . . It implies that absolutely nothing exists which does not comply with the law of cause and effect . . .

Karma means action, work or deed, and in terms of spiritual development, it refers to all that a person has done, is doing, and will do.

Welcome to the Karma Café. There are no menus. You will get served what you deserve.

—*Anonymous*

Karma is defined differently among Buddhists and various schools of Hinduism but a common theme across them all is the principle of causality— that each person is responsible for his or her own life, and how they treat other people through their actions and intentions affects the life he or she lives.

At its core, karma is about personal development and learning the lessons we need to learn in life so that we can become better people. It's about the energy we put out into the world and knowing that our thoughts and actions affect not only us but everyone and everything around us.

The catalyst for sending good energy into the world is gratitude, and the way to create good karma is through our positive actions. Through them, you not only create good karma, you also condition yourself and those around you to experience greater peace and happiness.

We each have the unique ability to bring greater joy into our life and the lives of others through the actions and interactions we engage in every day of our lives. Below are four steps you can follow to increase the good karma in your life.

STEP 1: PRACTICE KINDNESS

Have compassion and be kind. Many cultures around the world teach a basic philosophy that most of us call the *"Golden Rule"*—the concept of *do unto others as you would have them do unto you.*

It's called the *golden rule* for a reason—it promotes kindness, compassion, and understanding among people, all of which leads to good karma. After all, does it really make a difference what your culture is, where you were born, what country you live in, what your skin color is, or whether you're rich or poor? We all want pretty much the same things in life—to be treated with respect, to avoid pain and suffering, and to have health, happiness, security, love and affection for ourselves, our friends and our families, for our planet and all its inhabitants, large and small. Most people the world over are also fearful of the same things—becoming ill, not being to afford the things they need or want, being alone or lonely, and ultimately, dying and leaving the people and things they love behind.

At the end of the day, we're all in this thing called life together. And one day we're each going to die. The great unknowns are how, when, and where. What is in our power however, is how we use the gift of life that we've been given.

Everyone the world over is dependent on each other in one way or another, so it makes sense that showing kindness and compassion to each other should be a primary concern for each of us. If we think only of ourselves and fail to see that we're part of a greater whole, happiness will elude us. But when we move from a preoccupation with ourselves to a concern for the welfare and well-being of the extended human family and our planet as a whole, we'll develop what the Dalai Lama calls *"the good heart,"*— the desire to help others.

One of the best ways to send good karma into the world is to live with kindness and compassion. It doesn't matter if it's directed at family, friends, strangers, animals, or the environment—or whether your actions are direct or anonymous. What's important is to practice acts of kindness. And one of the best people to start practicing this with is yourself.

STEP 2: BE GOOD TO YOURSELF

Low self-esteem, self-doubt, and self-blame are unfortunately, part of being human. If you focus more on what you don't like about yourself, or what you do wrong, now is as good a time as any to give some serious thought about what is good in your life and what is good about you.

When times are tough, instead of beating yourself up, be the friend or mentor you wish you had. What advice would you give a friend who came to you with the same issues or problems you may be wrestling with? If you find yourself being harder on yourself than you would be on your friend, give yourself a break and show yourself the same love, compassion and forgiveness you would offer them. To quote Ralph Waldo Emerson: *nothing can bring you peace but yourself. So, make peace with yourself.* Be gentle and kind to the most important person in your life—*you.*

STEP 3: SHOW EMPATHY

If someone has wronged you or hurt you emotionally, it's not always easy to forgive and forget, but according to Christopher Peterson, one of the founding fathers of positive psychology, *forgiveness is the trait most strongly linked to happiness.*

The next time you find yourself in a challenging situation with someone, take a deep breath, relax, and try to see it from their point of view. Maybe they're having a hard day and could use some understanding or a helping hand from a compassionate person like you who won't hold their words or actions against them. Imagine yourself in their shoes and think how you may have reacted if you were him or her. More often than not, if you can reverse the roles you're each playing, you can step out of the anger zone and see things from a calmer and more compassionate perspective.

By modeling behaviors of insight and forgiveness you can set an example for them and others to follow. Things don't always go the way we've planned, and people don't always act the way we expect. When that happens, remember the wise words of Mahatma Gandhi: *Be the change you want to see in the world."*

STEP 4: LIVE AUTHENTICALLY

Your karma, good or bad, will reflect the values you choose in life. As you'll recall from the chapter on GOALS, the first

"G" in the GLAD formula, your values should guide the goals you choose to pursue. Choose your values wisely as they form the foundation of your character and reputation and will create your karma in the world.

Be honest. Live with integrity. Be the best person you can possibly be. Show kindness and compassion and help others along your life's journey. When your thoughts, words and actions are consistent with your values, you'll live a life that's authentic and will experience greater levels of happiness in all areas of your life.

G^{3}LA^{2}D: 7 PRINCIPLES FOR A HAPPIER LIFE

LET IT GO

> Look at life
> through the windshield,
> not the rear-view mirror.
>
> —*Byrd Baggert*

We've all been there. Someone has angered us, wronged us, said something unfair or untrue, or hurt us in some way that we just can't or won't forgive. And why should we? After all, they're the ones who acted badly, not us. They're the ones creating bad karma for themselves. All we did was react to their bad energy which shouldn't affect our karma, right? Well… not really. Remember that the key is to avoid bad energy as much as possible, whether it comes from other people or from ourselves. Responding in a negative way or hoping that life is going to "get even" with them for us is the same as sending out bad energy—*bad Karma,* to the universe.

A healthier way to live a happier life is to let go of whatever unhealthy attachments you may have to people, ideas, things, or events that caused or are causing you stress. This is important not only for your own peace of mind but for your overall health in general since forgiving and "letting go" of hurts and wrongs is something research has shown benefits you. According to Sonja Lyubomirsky, the positive psychologist and happiness researcher I referenced earlier: *Empirical research confirms this insight: Forgiving people are less likely to be hateful, depressed, hostile, anxious, angry, and neurotic. They are more likely to be happier, healthier, more agreeable, and more serene.*

If you're holding on to grudges or acting like a victim in any part of your life, expressing gratitude becomes more and more challenging, but also more important, to do. While it's admittedly easier said than done, sometimes you need to accept *what is* to let go of *what was.*

Whatever your age is now, know this: short or long, life comes with an expiration date. We just don't know what the date is. And every day you hold on to what you should be leaving behind is time wasted that could be better spent going after the goals you've decided will give your life meaning and happiness.

Charlotte Brontë, the English novelist and poet, wrote in her novel*, Jane Eyre: Life appears to me too short to be spent in nursing animosity or registering wrongs.* Brontë lived according to her philosophy and she was absolutely right about life being too short—she died of pneumonia just before her 39th birthday, but accomplished quite a lot in her short life, which included the world-famous novel *Jane Eyre.*

Whatever you're holding onto—whether it's anger, a grudge, guilt over something you did or didn't do, a dream you never followed, a relationship that ended badly, a lost friendship, a career you never went for—whatever it may be, if it's holding you in place like an anchor weighing you down, blocking your positive energy, and keeping you from moving toward the life you dream of having, then you need *to let it go.*

There is no one more responsible than you for who you are today or who you will be tomorrow. Not your parents, not your friends, no one. Every decision you've made, every action you've taken, and everything you thought, said, or did, was up to you. Whether or not you continue to allow yourself to hold onto or let go of situations or emotions that were, or are still causing you stress or pain, is now up to you. You can choose to be happy and live a life that brings you joy or you can hold onto past hurts and pain. The choice is yours.

There's a wise Cherokee parable called *Two Wolves* that illustrates this point so well that it's worth sharing. It goes like this:

An old Cherokee is teaching his grandson about life. "A fight is going on inside me," he said to the boy.

"It is a terrible fight and it is between two wolves. One is evil—he is anger, envy, sorrow, regret, greed, arrogance, self-pity, guilt, resentment, inferiority, lies, false pride, superiority, and ego."

He continued, "The other is good—he is joy, peace, love, hope serenity, humility, kindness, benevolence, empathy, generosity, truth, compassion, and faith. The same fight is going on inside you—and inside every other person, too."

The grandson thought about it for a minute and then asked his grandfather, "Which wolf will win?" The old Cherokee simply replied, "The one you feed."

Don't feed the evil wolf inside of you that's been holding you back in life, or he'll continue to "win." Let him go.

If you don't like something in your life, figure out a way to change it. And if you can't change it, then as hard as it may be, you may just need to accept it and move on. Tell yourself: *It is what it is. Things are what they are.*

Remember what we said earlier about loving and forgiving yourself? Letting go is an act of acceptance, which is an act of self-love. Choosing to let go of the pain in your life for the sake of your dreams, joy and happiness is the most loving thing you can do for yourself. You're the only one who can decide when the time is right to let go of the past to have a happier future. Make the decision to give yourself whatever love and compassion you need—and then, *let it go.*

SIX STEPS TO LET IT GO

1. Place a pen and paper or your mobile phone next to your bed before going to bed tonight. Before going to sleep, ask your subconscious mind to think about those issues that are causing you the most suffering or pain.

2. When you wake up, write down whatever you dreamed or thought about that has been weighing you down or holding you back in life. [Alternatively, find a small rock and imagine it represents whatever pain or hardships have been holding you back in life.]

3. Mark a date on your calendar to let go of those things that have been weighing you down. When the date comes, burn the paper, or feel a connection with the stone you selected, and

throw the stone as far away as possible. Wish the burnt ashes of paper, or the stone, well. Thank it for serving whatever purpose it served at those points in your life that you needed it.

4. Relax, breathe in and out slowly and calmly thinking about the issues you let go. You're now free of them. You've let them go.

5. Stay present. Keep your focus on the here and now. You no longer need to ruminate on the past or worry about the future.

6. Smile. You've taken a major positive step forward in your life.

Letting things go that have been holding you back for months or years is not easy. It takes introspection, honesty, compassion (for yourself and others), and a sincere desire to move forward with your life. But the most important quality, the one that will provide a solid foundation for those other qualities, can be summed up in one word: *Attitude.* With the right attitude almost everything is possible—which is why *Attitude* is the principle we'll be discussing next.

G^{3}LA^{2}D: 7 PRINCIPLES FOR A HAPPIER LIFE

ATTITUDE

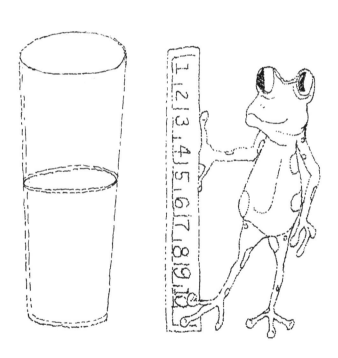

G^{3}LA^{2}D: 7 PRINCIPLES FOR A HAPPIER LIFE

> Attitude is a little thing
> that makes a big difference.
>
> —*Winston Churchill*

L ife is attitude. And everything you do or will do, from the smallest task on your to-do list to the major decisions you'll make in life, will be impacted, for better or worse, by your attitude.

One of the greatest principles to living a happier life, that we all seem to know but don't always live by, is that our attitude in any situation is *totally* under our control. We can choose to listen to self-defeating thoughts and negative self-talk, or we can choose to have an optimistic outlook and inner dialogue of positive words and self-encouragement. As Viktor Frankl so powerfully wrote when referring to the indignities suffered by concentration camp inmates: *Everything can be taken from a man but one thing: the last of the human freedoms - to choose one's attitude in any given set of circumstances, to choose one's own way.*

If the well-known saying "life is attitude" is true, then your thoughts — *what* you think about, and *how* you think about them, will determine your attitude, which in turn, will influence your actions in any situation you face, now or in the future.

As discussed, sometimes we just need to accept that things are the way they are and there's nothing we can do to change them. But getting to that point of acceptance often requires a change in attitude and the ability to see things from a different, more positive perspective. If you can train yourself to be more optimistic, to look for the positives when life throws problems your way and try to see everything that happens to you—good *and* bad, as a learning experience, you'll be better able to deal with life's inevitable ups and downs and see them as teaching opportunities that lead to your ongoing growth and development.

But what if you're just a born pessimist? What if you've always been someone who sees the glass half empty? Then what?

That's when you should remember the Cherokee parable and take control of the battling wolves inside your head. The most influential voice you hear day in and day out is your *own inner voice* and it will work for you or against you depending on which voice you listen to. With practice you can teach yourself to replace negative self-talk with constructive self-talk whenever you catch yourself thinking negatively. Feeding the good wolf will improve your attitude and help you see the glass half full.

By the way, this isn't just a cliché—research has shown that a key ingredient of happiness is an ability to appreciate the positive experiences in your life by remembering and reflecting on happy times and experiences from your past, feeling grateful for the good things you currently have, and thinking about and anticipating the positive things you can look forward to in the future.

Training yourself to be more optimistic—to have a more positive attitude, is not only good for your mind, it's also good for your health. According to Dr.'s Southwick and Charney, authors of *Resilience—The Science of Mastering Life's Greatest Challenges:*

- Optimists developed fewer stress-related psychological illnesses, such as Post-Traumatic Stress Disorder (PTSD) and depression.

- Those who were optimistic had a significantly lower risk of dying from cardiovascular problems than those who were pessimistic.

- Of all the variables, only positive emotion was related to longevity.

- Even if you are a born pessimist, or a very limited situational optimist, you can teach yourself to increase optimistic thought.

When you think about it, you pretty much only have two options when you're faced with something you don't like— you can try to change the situation, or you can change how you deal with it. If you can change the situation, then great, go ahead and change it for the better. But usually, the easiest and more effective option isn't to change the world around you, it's to change how you deal with the world.

Your attitude, more than most anything else, will determine whether you will deal positively or negatively with whatever comes your way. Ralph Waldo Emerson had it right when he wrote, *"Though we travel the world over to find the beautiful, we must carry it with us or we find it not."*

We can't always control what happens to us, but we can control how we react to situations no matter how tough those situations might be.

If you want to change something—whether it's how you feel, how you interact with someone or something, or what you believe, try switching your thoughts and reframing how you view the situation.

The scientific name for adjusting our attitude is cognitive reframing, and it's done by finding a more positive interpretation, view, or experience of unexpected adverse events, concepts, or ideas we don't like.

The next time you're confronted with a negative situation or someone or something that challenges your self-confidence, makes you feel you're not up to the

> If you don't like something, change it. If you can't change it, change the way you think about it.
> — *Mary Engelbreit*

task, or just plain scares you, take the following steps:

1. **DESCRIBE THE SITUATION AS ACCURATELY AS POSSIBLE**

    Our negative thoughts like to see reality as darker than it really is, especially when we experience something negative. With cognitive reframing, the first step is to make sure you're perceiving the situation as clearly and accurately as possible by making a fair assessment of the negatives and positives without irrational beliefs or cognitive distortions.

2. **ASSESS YOUR ABILITY TO DEAL WITH THE SITUATION**

   Ask yourself: *What is the best way to deal with this kind of a situation? Are there ways I can turn this from a negative situation into a positive one?* Decide whether you have enough knowledge and skills to successfully handle the situation. If you do, be confident knowing you can deal with whatever needs to be done. If you don't, then figure out who you can go to or what information or skills you may need to learn to succeed at the challenge.

3. **EXPLORE DIFFERENT POINTS OF VIEW**

   Consider the situation from someone else's point of view and see how that might change your perspective. Challenging events and situations often result in something good over time. Ask yourself: *What went right? Are there any positives*

that can come out of this? Are there opportunities
I can learn and grow from? Are there other ways
I can think about this? How would other people
who I know and admire think about this?

Just to be clear—your goal isn't to deny the reality of the situation you're dealing with, but to see whatever you're facing a bit differently—to reframe your attitude so that you can:

- turn a problem into an opportunity
- turn a weakness into a strength
- understand the hurtful actions of others instead of being a victim or engaging in unpleasant interactions
- find an opportunity to learn and grow from the challenges that come your way

More often than not, when you're not happy, the best person to make things better for yourself is you. Stay focused on what you can control and don't get hung up on what you can't since there's not a whole lot you can do about it anyway. Reinhold Niebuhr's world-famous *Serenity Prayer* says it best: *God, grant me the serenity to accept the things I cannot change, the courage to change the things I can, and the wisdom to know the difference.*

And remember this proverb: *when the student is ready the teacher will appear.* When you start to see everything and everyone—*good or bad,* as a teacher from whom you can learn and grow, you'll change your attitude for the better and become a wiser and happier person for it.

EXERCISES TO HELP YOU
IMPROVE YOUR ATTITUDE

1. When you think negative events in your life will last forever (permanence thinking), will have a negative impact on all areas of your life (universality thinking), and you hear yourself using words like *always* or *never* when describing these events, then do the following: use words like *sometimes* or *lately* when talking about the events, view them as *temporary and limited in scope,* and tell yourself you have the ability and strength to change and positively influence the outcome of events in your life.

2. Challenge your negative self-talk and unhelpful thoughts to see if they're accurate. For example,

let's say you get lost when driving and you tell yourself, *"I'm so stupid—I never follow directions and always get lost."* Question your thoughts by proving to yourself that there have been times when you've successfully followed directions and gotten where you needed to go without getting lost. After challenging your negative thinking often enough, you'll see that your negative self-talk isn't accurate after all. And don't stop there—in addition to challenging your negative self-talk, don't forget to give yourself praise when you deserve it!

3. Replace negative thoughts with positive, realistic, success-oriented affirmations and thoughts. Read *The Power of Positive Thinking* by Norman Vincent Peale—over five million copies have been sold since it was first published and it's considered a classic

for a reason. Or listen to positive affirmation audio books to encourage and reinforce positive thoughts and messages.

4. Surround yourself with uplifting, happy people who are confident, encouraging, and positive. They'll raise the bar on how you think about yourself and their ongoing positive nature will rub off on you!

5. Take full responsibility for your life. When things don't turn out the way you planned, don't make excuses and don't see yourself as a victim. Ask yourself three questions: *a. what's the worst that could happen? b. what do I think will most likely happen? c. what can I realistically do that might improve what happens?*

6. Instead of avoiding problems, face up to them, learn and grow from your failures, and build whatever skills, knowledge and capabilities you need to tackle the goals you've set for yourself. And always remember: you don't need to be the best—you just need to be the best *you* that you can be.

Changing your attitude takes work and time but can be done if you keep an open mind, are willing to learn from the different experiences you'll have throughout your life, and when you believe your life can change for the better. In 1995, Dr. Wayne Dyer, the late psychologist, self-help author, and motivational speaker, wrote a book called, *You'll See it When You Believe It,* which made the case that we can use our mind to see and feel the positive in any situation and that we have the power within us to become whoever we want to be.

Dr. Dyer made an interesting and powerful case for this concept. But more importantly, the premise on which his book was based is supported by research. And it's the next principle coming up in *GLAD*.

G^{3}LA^{2}D: 7 PRINCIPLES FOR A HAPPIER LIFE

ACT AS IF

> I am not what happened to me.
> I am what I choose to become.
>
> —*Carl Jung*

Common sense tells you that emotions come before behavior. Which is why most self-help literature says that if you want to change your behavior you first need to change the way you think.

Going against the prevailing wisdom, James Laird, Professor of Psychology at Clark University in Worchester, MA., turned common sense thinking on its head in his book Feelings: *The Perceptions of the Self,* which documents his years of scientific research on emotion. Based on his hundreds of studies, Dr. Laird wrote that emotions, motivation, and other private feelings *are inferred from our behaviors* rather than being directly perceived. In plain English that means: emotions don't cause behavior—they *follow* from behavior.

A similar concept was proposed by Charles Darwin over one hundred years ago when he suggested that physiological changes weren't just the result of an emotion but could influence our emotions. This *facial feedback hypothesis* as it's come to be known, says that our facial expressions can have an effect on our emotional experiences—for example, that the simple behavioral choice to move our facial muscles into a smile is enough to make us *feel* happier. Studies have even shown that *acting as if you're happy* by smiling can help lower your heart rate during stressful activities. And according to a 2014 study published in the Journal of *Behavior Therapy and Experimental Psychiatry,* simply imitating the walking style of a happy person can help improve your mood.

Thinking along the same lines as Darwin, William James, the famous 19th century American philosopher and psychologist, hypothesized that the relationship between emotion and behavior was a two-way street and that behavior can cause emotion.

> If you want
> a quality,
> act as if you
> already had it.
> —*William James*

James believed that *doing* things could lead to changes in feelings. He wrote: *Human beings can alter their lives by altering their attitudes of mind. By regulating the action, which is under the more direct control of the will, we can indirectly regulate the feeling, which is not.*

James's advice to "act as if' became a guiding principle for many therapy programs since then, and his and Laird's research, along with other studies in the field of psychology, have provided empirical support for the theories put forward by Charles Darwin and William James as far back as the 1800's.

A more current example of "act as if" thinking can be found in an article published in the November-December 2016 issue of Harvard Magazine called, *Acting As If for 35 Seasons.* The article featured Harvard women's basketball coach Kathy Delaney-Smith, recognized as the all-time winningest Ivy League head coach in Ivy League men's and women's basketball history.

Delaney-Smith insisted that her accomplishments were not extraordinary, but were instead, the result of three words: *ACT AS IF*—which embodied her belief that performance is at least 80 percent mental. According to Delaney-Smith, *"act as if"* thinking involves convincing oneself that challenges can be overcome and goals are attainable.

In a film made about her, Delaney-Smith explained that she encouraged her players to *act as if* they're not tired, to *act as if* they're great shooters, and to *act as if* they were already the winners they wanted to be. Which is in essence a variation of, "fake it until you make it," a well-known saying which proposes that if you act in a certain way long enough, that behavioral pattern will become entrenched in your psyche and eventually become a part of who you are.

In a March 20, 2009 New York Times article called, *First Step in Becoming a Winner: Act Like One,* Melissa Johnson, a player on Delaney-Smith's Harvard basketball team, described how Delaney-Smith used the act as if concept. In her article, Johnson described her decision to transfer to Harvard from North Carolina after watching sixteenth-seeded Harvard beat top-ranked Stanford in the 1998 N.C.A.A. tournament. She wrote: *Wanting to learn from someone who could pull off this kind of magic, I transferred to play for her the next year, and she told me her secret. Any decent athlete, salesman or Starbucks barista can put on a good game face. But her philosophy, "act as if," goes much deeper than mere swagger or theatrics. It's a method—a learned skill for convincing your mind that you already are what you want to become. The body follows where the mind leads. "Act as if you're a great shooter," she would instruct. "Act as if you love the drill. Act as if when you hit the deck it doesn't hurt." Negativity, even in the form of body language, was not tolerated.*

The goal of "acting as if" is to create the conditions for what you want to make a reality in your life—whether it's acting as if you already have something you really want, acting as if something is already present in your life, or acting as if you know how to do something even though you may not yet know how.

The same theory applies to your feelings—when your actions are consistent with a particular feeling, those feelings will eventually become a part of you. By the way, since this theory holds for both positive *and* negative emotions, it's important that your behaviors reflect the "act as if" outcome you're looking for—the *positive* emotions.

More than seventy years before Wayne Dyer wrote his book *You'll See it When You Believe It,* Alfred Adler, the famous Austrian doctor, psychotherapist, and founder of the school of individual psychology, encouraged the acting as if technique in the 1920's when he counseled his clients to act as if they were already the person they would like to be—say, a "confident individual."

If William James, James Laird, Wayne Dyer, Alfred Adler, and other researchers, motivational speakers and psychologists who study the field of emotions and behavior are right, then by behaving a certain way (e.g., confident, optimistic, outgoing, or happy), you can experience the same feelings you would experience

> Life isn't about finding yourself. Life is about creating yourself.
> —*Anonymous*

if you were that way. Just keep in mind that "acting as if" is not the same as just thinking or visualizing what you want to be true.

You need to act as though the behaviors you want to own are already your reality. And when you do that, acting as if will make your actions consistent with your beliefs and bring the power of your thoughts and intentions together in a meaningful way so that your emotions reflect your behavior.

We really shouldn't find the "act as if" concept all that surprising since we play different characters in our lives all the time—we play the role of employee, friend, daughter, son, or neighbor, and "act" the way each of those roles require us to act. The technique of *acting as if* just gives you another opportunity to consciously become the person you'd like to be.

Act as if and the feelings will follow. You'll *become* different when you start *acting as if* you are different.

EXERCISES TO MAKE "ACT AS IF" THINKING A REALITY

1. List two or three of your most inspiring role models, either current or historical, and note a few traits about each of them that you admire:

    _____

    _____

2. Now write down two or three situations that you'll be dealing with soon or in the near future that you think will make you anxious or unsure of yourself.

    _____

    _____

    _____

3. Pick one of the role models from your list whom you admire most. Write down in as much detail as you can how your role model would act in those situations. How would they dress? How would they walk and move? How would they talk and behave? What words, tone, or expressions would they use when interacting with the people you'll come into contact with?

_____

_____

_____

4. Imagine yourself being that person and *acting* the way he or she would act given the characteristics you outlined above. *See it. Feel it. Be it.*

5. Mentally rehearse those ways of acting when you're faced with similar situations in the future. Then act the part and believe this person is you.

6. Support your new way of being by acquiring whatever new knowledge and/or skills you need to help you become the person you're trying to become. Over time, you'll find that the feelings associated with the role you've been playing will become more and more a part of who you are.

The exercises above and the other exercises in *GLAD* can help you make positive changes in your life, but only if you're willing to put in the effort to make change happen.

If you're serious about improving your life, you'll need to take action to make it happen. In 1737, Benjamin Franklin wrote: *Well done is better than well said.* You may have also heard a more current and similar expression: *Actions speak louder than words.* Both sayings advise the same thing— there comes a time when we need to stop talking and start doing. Which is the topic of our next and final *GLAD* principle: *Do It.*

DO IT

> The way to get started
> is to quit talking and
> begin doing.
>
> — *Walt Disney*

L et's kick off this final principle with a riddle: *Five frogs are sitting on a log. Four decide to jump off. How many are left?*

If you guessed *one*, then you'll find this section helpful, because the correct answer is five. Why five? Because there's a big difference between *deciding* to do something and *doing* it.

Think back to the first *GLAD* principle—choosing a purposeful *GOAL* or goals that are aligned with your values and give purpose to your life. As important as it is to develop personal and meaningful goals, you'll need a well-thought-out plan to accomplish the goals you've decided will add meaning to your life because the best advice in the world won't do you any good if you don't put what you learn into action.

And no one but you can do it for you.

When asked, most people have no problem coming up with a list of life goals for themselves. But for one reason or another, many of their goals never get realized.

> You can't build a reputation on what you're *going* to do.
> — *Henry Ford*

They lose their focus or interest, give up before they get started, or don't really want what they thought they wanted. Or maybe the timing isn't right, or they don't have the skills they think they need to accomplish their goals, or they let a fear of failure stop them. Whatever the reason, their goals

134

get moved to the *"one day when I have more time I'll do this"* list. The late Jim Rohn, author and motivational speaker said: *If you really want to do something, you will find a way. If you don't, you will find an excuse.*

Don't find an excuse. If you've been putting off working on areas of your life that have been on your mind for longer than you'd like to admit—whether it's tackling the goals on your bucket list, deciding to let go of past pains and hurts, or taking up meditation and yoga to find greater peace of mind, then take this Chinese proverb to heart: *The best time to plant a tree was twenty years ago. The second-best time is now.*

This applies to each of the *GLAD* principles we've covered—whether it's appreciating all the good things you have to be grateful for in your life, taking positive actions that build up your good karma, letting things go that have been keeping you from moving forward, or reframing your attitude when issues or challenges come your way, you will need *to do something*—to take some form of action to live according to these principles.

> Don't wish for it. Work for it.
> —*Anonymous*

Yes, applying the *GLAD* principles to your life will take effort, but the payoff for your health and long-term happiness will be worth it. You'll experience a greater sense of purpose, enjoyment and happiness when you follow the principles in *GLAD*. As Brian Tracy wrote in *Goals! How to Get Everything You Want—Faster Than You Ever Thought Possible:* "A goal or a decision without a deadline is merely a wish." So, the two questions you need to ask yourself are: *1) Will living the GLAD principles bring me more fulfillment and happiness?* If your answer is YES, then you need to ask:

2) What can I start doing today that will change my life for the better?

Below are some questions to help you get started. When answering them, keep in mind the words of Thomas Edison, a true visionary who represents *Do It* as much, if not more, than anyone else in modern history: *What you are will show in what you do.*

QUESTIONS TO HELP YOU "DO IT"

1. A year from now what will you wish you had done today that will have the most positive impact on your life?

   _____

2. What potential obstacles—real or imagined, are keeping you from doing them?

---

3. For each of the GLAD principles below, write at least one action you can take this week that will make a meaningful difference in your life.

GOALS: What central purpose can you build your life around that is aligned with your values and will give your life direction and meaning?

GRATITUDE: Each week, starting this Sunday night, write down 3-5 things you were grateful for that week.

GOOD KARMA: Commit to at least one thing you can do for someone this coming week—either someone you know or a total stranger, that will create positive energy and good Karma.

_____

LET IT GO: List whatever grudges or resentments you may be holding onto that have been keeping you from having peace, comfort, and happiness in your life—then do the exercises in the Let It Go chapter to help you move on from them.

_____

ATTITUDE: Choose three areas of your life that are being impacted by your negative thinking. Write down two ways that you can reframe each negative into a positive.

_____

ACT AS IF: Consider how you would think, move, talk, and interact with yourself or other people if you reframed your negatives into the positives listed above. Beginning today, start acting as if this was your reality.

_____

DO IT: Each day for the next three weeks, review your answers to the questions above and commit to following through on your answers.

WRAPPING UP

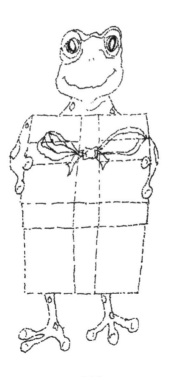

G^{3}LA^{2}D: 7 PRINCIPLES FOR A HAPPIER LIFE

> You practice
> and you get better.
> It's very simple.
> —*Philip Glass*

A s we've learned, a happy life doesn't come from chasing temporary pleasures or material things, since more often than not, they only make us happier in the short-term. Long-lasting happiness comes from living a life with purpose and direction, expressing gratitude for what's good in our life, sending good karma into the world, having the right attitude toward whatever challenges, disappointments, or setbacks may come our way, and doing things in life that create happiness instead of passively waiting for happiness to come our way.

Building a life of meaning, fulfillment, and happiness is an ongoing journey that needs time and effort from you. And since the journey is happiness, we also know that happiness is not a destination you reach but is something you experience, and keep experiencing along the way, when you're living a life of meaning, compassion, and purpose.

Living the *GLAD* principles takes work but isn't any more difficult than the habits you may have developed in other areas of your life like exercising, eating healthy food, or following an ongoing regimen of good hygiene.

The good news is that it won't take you long to build the *GLAD* principles into your daily way of living. *"GLAD"* is easy to remember, so when you think about the core principles that spell *GLAD*, you'll be able to review and apply them to your life when appropriate situations come up. Practice the principles until they become a habit and soon they'll guide your thoughts, actions and decisions when-ever you need them.

Conventional thinking used to be that it takes 21 days for a new behavior to become a habit, but research by Phillippa Lally, a health psychology researcher at University College London, published a study in the *European Journal of Social Psychology* that showed it takes a bit longer before a new behavior becomes automatic—about two months, or 66 days more or less, depending on the person, the circumstances, and the behavior. What her research also found is that building good habits is not an all-or-nothing process—which means that even if you mess up now and then by not always sticking to the principle you were hoping to follow, it won't seriously impact the habit formation process.

> Be not afraid of going slowly. Be only afraid of standing still.
> — *Chinese Proverb*

Practice living the *GLAD* principles as often as you can and they'll soon become an essential part of your approach to life. And remember that each principle impacts and influences the others—working on one of the *GLAD* principles leads naturally to the other principles.

For example, after you've done the necessary soul-searching and decided on personally meaningful *goals* for yourself, you'll feel *grateful* that you found something that gives direction and purpose to your life. The gratitude you feel creates good energy, which leads to positive actions that create *good Karma,* which brings more positive things your way to feel grateful about. To keep your karma positive, you'll work on *letting things go* that have been holding you back—and to let things go, you'll know that sometimes you need to change your *attitude* on how you view less than positive areas of your life that have been keeping you from moving forward. If you need help with your attitude, you'll

146

use *"act as if"* thinking to kick-start those changes you'd like to bring into your life. And to make and keep making progress in all of these principles, you'll take action—you'll *"Do It,"* since the only person who can make things happen for you is you.

In closing, I'd like to remind you of the promise I made in the introduction to *GLAD*: if you're looking to have a more satisfying life, are willing to follow the principles presented in *GLAD*, and will take the time to do some (if not all) of the exercises at the end of each section, you will be a happier person and have better tools to deal with the ups and downs of life after reading *GLAD* than you had before.

Not only do I believe you'll be a happier person for having incorporated the *GLAD* principles into your life, but by becoming a more fulfilled and happier person yourself, you'll make your extended world of family, friends, social connections, and society, a better and happier place.

I'll end this final chapter with a quote from the Dalai Lama, the leading authority on how to live a good and compassionate life, who wrote: *"individual happiness can contribute in a profound and effective way to the overall improvement of our entire human community."*

If there's a more worthwhile reason than that to improve our own personal happiness, I can't imagine what it would be.

APPENDIX

MEDITATION

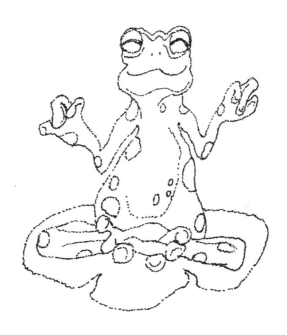

If you are quiet enough, you will hear the flow
of the universe. You will feel its rhythm.
Go with this flow. Happiness lies ahead.
Meditation is key.
— *Buddha*

E ach day seems to bring new stresses, distractions, and demands on our time. Most of us could benefit by letting our thoughts relax, being less anxious and judgmental, and finding a way to calm and refresh our minds to keep our lives and the challenges we need to deal with in balance and in perspective.

Wouldn't it be great if there was a way to bring our thoughts to a state of concentration and insight that would not only help us make better decisions but would also lead to a happier life?

Say hello to the age-old practice of meditation.

The benefits of meditation as a way to adjust our physical and mental well-being are well documented and have been shown to have a significant impact on our health, from reducing stress and lowering blood pressure, to strengthening our immune system and increasing our brain development. And, if clearing your mind and calming you down aren't reasons enough to start meditating, the fact that studies have shown that it's one of the most effective ways to live a happier life might just do the trick.

For our purposes, meditation, with its goal of focusing awareness, can help you think through and make the best decisions possible when following the seven *GLAD* principles—from developing your goals and helping you appreciate all the things you have to be grateful for, to knowing what you should let go of that's not working for you and when to reframe your attitude for the better. Meditation can help you focus your awareness on each of the *GLAD* principles so that you can live a more satisfying and happier life.

There are as many books and apps about meditation as there are ways to do it, so to save you some time, outlined below are key steps to get you started.

A FIVE-STEP MEDITATION PRIMER

1. CHOOSE A PEACEFUL PLACE

The place you choose to meditate doesn't have to be large. It should however, be private, quiet, and relaxing, with as few distractions as possible. (Don't forget to turn off your phone, TV, or other devices before you start to meditate.)

2. SIT COMFORTABLY

You don't have to sit cross-legged in a traditional lotus pose. The goal is to focus your awareness on your mind and not your body, so feel free to sit in a way that's natural and comfortable. Sit on a cushion if you'd like, keep your back straight (but not tense), keep your shoulders level and your elbows held slightly away from your sides. Then place your hands comfortably on top of your lap.

3. BREATHE MINDFULLY

Keep your eyes either closed or half open and gazing down along the line of your nose. The intent is not to fall asleep but to feel relaxed, yet alert. Touch your tongue against the back of your upper teeth and breathe in naturally through your nose to a count of four. Pause, then exhale slowly through your nose to a count of six.

4. FOCUS ON YOUR BREATHING

Breathe normally. Stay aware of the rising and falling of your stomach as you breathe in and out. Don't worry if you get restless and your thoughts wander—when they do, just refocus on your breathing until your mind quiets down. If it helps you to focus, think about a visual object (a coin on your stomach that goes up and down with each breath and exhalation, or the flame of a lit candle), or repeat a mantra (a sound or word such as "ŌM" or a phrase that is calming and peaceful to you) over and over to yourself whenever your mind begins to drift off. When your mind wanders, don't stress about it—just refocus on your breathing or repeat your mantra.

5. DON'T OVERPRACTICE

Sitting still for any length of time isn't easy, so start your practice slowly for about five minutes at a time. If you can meditate at the same time every day, it won't take long before it becomes part of your daily routine. Early morning is usually a good time to meditate since you're not stressed yet from the day ahead. Decide how long you'd like to meditate and then set a timer or practice for the length of a relaxing, instrumental song or soundtrack. After you've become comfortable meditating for short periods, try working yourself up to 20 minutes a day. Before long, you'll know how long it takes you to calm down, relax, and quiet your mind.

Like happiness, meditation is a journey that takes time and practice to realize its full benefits.

You'll know it's working when you start focusing more on solutions than problems, you begin feeling less anxious or reactive, and you begin appreciating things that you once took for granted. But best of all, if you put in the time, meditation will give you the awareness and insights you'll need to more fully benefit from each of the *GLAD* principles.

INSPIRING QUOTES

> Colors fade,
> temples crumble,
> empires fall, but
> wise words endure.
>
> —*Agnes Sybil Thorndike*

I'm a quote collector and always have been. Over the years, I've learned that the right quote at the right time can work magic. They can help reframe your attitude, give you comfort or solace when needed, and can make you smile when you need it most.

A good selection of quotes is like having the wisdom of the world's most knowledgeable, experienced, and wisest friends on hand whenever you need them. They make their point clearly and concisely, are memorable, and can give you valued insight across all areas of life, which is why I've used them liberally when writing *GLAD*.

As additional support for each of the seven principles covered in *GLAD*, I've listed below some of my favorite quotes for you to refer back to whenever you need them most.

GOALS

The tragedy in life doesn't lie in not reaching your goal.

The tragedy lies in having no goal to reach.

— *Benjamin Mays*

An aim in life is the only fortune worth finding.

— *Robert Louis Stevenson*

What is purpose? The ONE Thing you want your life

to be about more than any other.

—*Gary Keller*

People with goals succeed because they know

where they are going. It is as simple as that.

— *Earl Nightingale*

A life without goals is like a race without a finish line.

— *Anonymous*

Goals give you that sense of meaning and purpose,
a clear sense of direction.

— *Brian Tracy*

If you don't know where you are going, you'll end up
some place else.

— *Yogi Berra*

The greatest tragedy in life is to spend your whole
life fishing only to discover that it was not fish you
 were after.

— *Henry David Thoreau*

Ever more people today have the means to live,
but no meaning to live for.

— *Viktor E. Frankl*

All life is a purposeful struggle, and your only choice
is the choice of a goal.

— *John Galt (Atlas Shrugged)*

There is one quality that one must possess to win,
and that is definiteness of purpose, the knowledge
of what one wants, and a burning desire to achieve it.

— *Napoleon Hill*

Happiness is the progressive realization of a
worthy ideal, or goal.

— *Earl Nightingale*

GRATITUDE

Happiness comes when we stop complaining about the troubles we have and offer thanks for all the troubles we don't have.

— *Anonymous*

When I started counted my blessings, my whole life turned around.

—*Willie Nelson*

There aren't that many things that interest me, but I'm fascinated by everything.

— *Luis Flores*

Write it on your heart that every day is the best day in the year.

—*Ralph Waldo Emerson*

Reflect on your present blessings, on which every man has many, not on your past misfortunes, of which all men have some.

—*Charles Dickens*

Feeling gratitude and not expressing it is like wrapping a present and not giving it."

—*William Arthur Ward*

Do not spoil what you have by desiring what you have not; remember that what you now have was once among the things you only hoped for.

—*Epicurus*

When asked if my cup is half-full or half-empty my only response is that I am thankful I have a cup.

— *Sam Lefkowitz*

My advice to you is not to inquire why or whither,
but just enjoy your ice cream while it's on your plate.
—*Thornton Wilder*

At the age of 18, I made up my mind to never have
another bad day in my life. I dove into an endless sea
of gratitude from which I've never emerged.
—*Patch Adams*

GOOD KARMA

When you choose the behavior, you choose

the consequences.

—*Phillip C. McGraw, PH.D.*

I am not a product of my circumstances. I am a product

of my decisions.

— *Stephen Covey*

It's not necessary to say everything you think,

but it is necessary to think about everything you say.

— *Quino*

The force of character is cumulative.

— *Ralph Waldo Emerson*

Without kindness, there can be no true joy.

—*Thomas Carlyle*

Always do your best. What you plant now,

you will harvest later.

— Og Mandino

It is not in the stars to hold our destiny

but in ourselves.

— William Shakespeare

How wonderful it is that nobody need wait a single

moment before starting to improve the world.

— Ann Frank

How people treat you is their karma;

how you react is yours.

—Wayne Dyer

I'm creating my future with every word,

every action, every thought.

— Pema Chodron

LET IT GO

In the process of letting go you will lose many things from the past, but you will find yourself.

—*Deepak Chopra*

To heal a wound you need to stop touching it.

—*Anonymous*

Holding onto anger is like drinking poison and expecting the other person to die.

—*Variously ascribed*

Failure is an education. It educates you by telling you that something is not working, that it is time to try something new, time to make an adjustment.

— *Kuehl*

You can't cling to the past if you want to create
the future.

— *Delta Airlines promo*

Losing an illusion makes you wiser than finding
a truth.

—*Ludwig Börne*

The greatest weapon against stress is our ability
to choose one thought over another.

— *William James*

Life = change. If you're changing anyway, why not change
for the better? Better or worse are your only choices;
you can't stay where you are forever.

— *Pete Koerner*

Don't cry because it's over. Smile because it happened.

—*Dr. Seuss*

You will continue to suffer if you have an emotional reaction to everything that is said to you. True power is sitting back and observing things with logic. True power is restraint. If words control you that means everyone else can control you. Breathe and allow things to pass.

—Anonymous

Forgive others, not because they deserve forgiveness, but because you deserve peace.

—Jonathan Lockwood Huie

Finish each day and be done with it. You have done what you could. Some blunders and absurdities have crept in; forget them as soon as you can. Tomorrow is a new day. You shall begin it serenely and with too high a spirit to be encumbered with your old nonsense.

—Ralph Waldo Emerson

ATTITUDE

If you don't like something, change it. If you can't change it, change your attitude.

—*Maya Angelou*

Things turn out best for those who make the best of the way things turn out.

— *Art Linkletter*

Most folks are usually about as happy as they make their minds up to be.

— *Abraham Lincoln*

It's not what happens to you, but how you react to it that matters.

— *Epictetus*

G³LA²D: 7 PRINCIPLES FOR A HAPPIER LIFE

An optimist sees an opportunity in every calamity;

A pessimist sees a calamity in every opportunity.

— *Sir Winston Churchill*

There are no wrong turns, only unexpected paths.

— *Mark Nepo*

I'm convinced that life is 10% of what happens to me

and 90% how I react to it.

— *Charles Swindoll*

Change the way you look at things and the things

you look at change.

—*Wayne Dyer*

Sometimes we succeed, sometimes we fail, but every day

is a clean slate and a fresh start.

— *Gretchin Rubin*

Though we travel the world over to find the beautiful, we must carry it with us or we find it not.

— *Ralph Waldo Emerson*

Difficulties come not to obstruct but to instruct.

— *Brian Tracy*

Do the best you can and don't take it so seriously.

— *Bernie Glassman*

Courage is going from failure to failure without losing enthusiasm.

— *Winston Churchill*

We either make ourselves miserable, our we make ourselves strong. The amount of work is the same.

— *Carlos Castaneda*

The greatest discovery of my generation is that a human being can alter his life by altering his attitude.

— *William James*

The mind is its own place, and in itself can make

a Heaven of Hell, a Hell of Heaven."

—*John Milton, Paradise Lost*

Difficult roads often lead to beautiful destinations.

—*Zig Ziglar*

Change your thoughts and you change your world.

—*Rev. Norman Vincent Peale*

ACT AS IF

Thought is the sculptor who can create the person you want to be.

—*Henry David Thoreau*

Begin to be now what you will be hereafter.

— *William James*

The chief happiness for a man is to be what he is.

— *Erasmus*

Go confidently in the direction of your dreams!

Live the life you've imagined.

— *Thoreau*

With our thoughts we make the world.

— *Buddha*

A musician must make music, an artist must paint,
a poet must write. If he is to be ultimately at peace
with himself, what a man can be, he must be.

— *Abraham Maslow*

Become who you are by learning who you are.

— *Pindar*

Everyone sees what you appear to be, few experience
what you really are.

— *Niccolò Machiavelli*

Treat people as if they were what they ought to be
and you help them to become what they are capable
of being.

— *Goethe*

My life didn't please me, so I created my life.

—*Coco Chanel*

It is never too late to be what you might have been.

— *George Eliot*

Knowing yourself is the beginning of all wisdom.

—*Aristotle*

I am not what happened to me, I am what I choose
to become.

—*Carl Jung*

DO IT

My success is due more to my ability to work continuously on one thing without stopping than to any other single quality.

—*Thomas Edison*

If you love life don't waste time. For time is what life is made of.

— *Bruce Lee*

He has half the deed done who has made a beginning.

— *Horace*

You miss 100 percent of the shots you don't take.

— *Wayne Gretzky*

You can't cross the sea by staring at the waves.

— *Anonymous*

All know the Way, but few actually walk it.

— *Bodhidharma*

Those who practice, improve. Those who don't, don't.

— *John Seery*

Work on one thing at a time until finished.

— *Henry Miller*

Do not act as if you had a thousand years to live.

—*Marcus Aurelius*

If you really wanted to you would.

— *Anonymous*

One day you will wake up and there won't be any more time to do the things you've always wanted to do. Do them now!

— *Paulo Coelho*

Enjoy life. It has an expiration date.

— *cafepress.com*

He who is not courageous enough to take risks

will accomplish nothing in life.

— *Muhammed Ali*

You are what you do, not what you say you'll do.

— *C.G. Jung*

Well done is better than well said.

— *Benjamin Franklin*

Knowing alone does not make us wise... it's not about what

we know, but what we do with that knowledge.

— *Timber Hawkeye*

It is not what you say, or wish, or hope or intend,

it is only what you do that counts.

— *Brian Tracy*

Inspiration is for amateurs. The rest of us just show up and get to work.

— *Chuck Close*

Happiness is not something ready-made. It comes from your own actions.

—*The Dalai Lamai*

RECOMMENDED READING

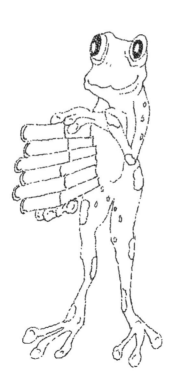

G^{3}LA^{2}D: 7 PRINCIPLES FOR A HAPPIER LIFE

I like exploring the titles of books in the self-help section of bookstores and on amazon.com to see what I can learn about life in general and how I can improve myself in particular. My library has been steadily growing over the years, and though the self-help books I've read haven't all been life changing, I usually take away some insights that are interesting, helpful, or thought provoking and referenced many of them in the writing of *GLAD*.

With the hope that some of the books I've found helpful might interest you, I've listed below a few titles about life, happiness, and life philosophy that will add to your knowledge, stimulate your thinking, and help you reflect on what's most important in life.

Enjoy!

Bridges, William. Transitions: Making Sense of Life's Changes. Cambridge, MA: Da Capo Press, 2014.

Carnegie, Dale. How to Stop Worrying and Start Living: Time-Tested Methods for Conquering Worry. New York: Gallery Books (Revised Edition), 2004.

Carlson, Richard, Ph.D. Don't Sweat the Small Stuff... and it's all small stuff. Simple Ways to Keep the Little Things from Taking Over Your Life. New York: MJF Books, 1997.

Chödrön, Pema. Taking the Leap: Freeing Ourselves from Old Habits and Fears. Boston, MA: Shambhala Publications, Inc., 2009.

Csikszentmihalyi, Mihaly. FLOW: The Psychology of Optimal Experience. Steps Toward Enhancing the Quality of Life. New York: HarperPerennial, 1991.

Dyer, Wayne. You'll See It When You Believe It: The Way to Your Personal Transformation. New York: William Morrow Paperbacks, 2001.

Frankl, Viktor E. Man's Search for Meaning. Boston, MA: Beacon Press, 2006

García, Héctor, and Miralles, Francesc. IKIGAI: The Japanese Secret to a Long and Happy Life. New York: Penguin Books, 2016.

Hawkeye, Timber. Buddhist Boot Camp. New York: HarperOne, 2013.

Izzo, John, Ph.D. The Five Secrets You Must Discover Before You Die. San Francisco: Berrett-Koehler Publications, Inc., 2008.

Keller, Gary, and Papasan, Jay. The ONE Thing: The Surprisingly Simple Truth Behind Extraordinary Results. Austin, Texas: Bard Press, 2013.

Lelord, François. Hector and the Search for Happiness. New York: Penguin Books, 2010.

Luna, Elle. The Crossroads of Should and Must: Find and Follow Your Passion. New York: Workman Publishing, 2015.

Lyubomirsky, Sonja. The How of Happiness: A New Approach to Getting the Life You Want. New York: Penguin Books, 2008.

McGraw, Phillip C., PH.D. Self Matters: Creating Your Life From the Inside Out. New York: Free Press, 2003.

McKeown, Greg. Essentialism: The Disciplined Pursuit of Less. New York: Crown Business, 2014.

Meisner, Sanford. On Acting. New York: Vintage Books, 1987.

Nhat Hanh, Thich. You Are Here: Discovering the Magic of the Present Moment. Boston, MA: Shambhala Publications, Inc., 2001.

Nightingale, Earl. The Strangest Secret. USA: Merchant Books, 2013.

Roger, John, and McWilliams, Peter. DO IT!: Let's Get Off Our Buts. Los Angeles, CA: Prelude Press, 1991

Rosman, Jonathan P., M.D., The Art of Joyful Living: A Practical Guide to Happiness. USA: Outskirts Press, Inc., 2013.

Sher, Barbara. I Could Do Anything If I Only Knew What It Was: How to discover what you really want and how to get it. New York: Dell, 1995.

Sincero, Jen. You are a Badass: How to Stop Doubting Your Greatness and Start Living an Awesome Life. Philadelphia, PA: Running Press, 2013.

Stanislavski, Constantin. An Actor Prepares. New York: Routledge, 1989.

Tracy, Brian. GOALS!: How to Get Everything You Want— Faster Than You Ever Thought Possible. San Francisco, CA: Berrett-Koehler Publishers, Inc., 2010

BIBLIOGRAPHY

.

Achor, Shawn. The Happiness Advantage: The Seven Principles of Positive Psychology That Fuel Success and Performance at Work. New York: Crown Business, 2010.

Aubele, Teresa, PhD, Wenck, Stan, EdD, and Reynolds, Susan. Train Your Brain To Get Happy: The Simple Program That Primes Your Gray Cells For Joy, Optimism, and Serenity. Avon, MA.: Adams Media, 2011.

Brickman, P., & Campbell, D. T. (1971). Hedonic relativism and planning the good society. In M.H. Apley (Ed.), Adaptation-level theory: A symposium (pp. 287-302). New York: Academic Press.

Browne, Harry, How I Found Freedom In An Unfree World. USA: Liam Works, 1998.

Buettner, Dan, The Blue Zones of Happiness: Lessons from the World's Happiest People: Washington, DC: National Geographic Partners, Inc., 2017.

Cooper, Belle Beth, "10 Simple Things You Can Do Today That Will Make You Happier, Backed By Science." 05 Nov 2016 http://blog.bufferapp.com/ 10-scientifically-proven-ways-to-make-yourself-happier.

Craig, Mary. The Pocket Dalai Lama. Boston, Massachusetts: Shambhala Publications, Inc., 2002.

Csikszentmihalyi, Mihaly. FLOW: The Psychology of Optimal Experience. Steps Toward Enhancing the Quality of Life. New York: HarperPerennial, 1991.

Elias, Marilyn, "Psychologists now know what makes people happy." USA Today December 8, 2002: Health and Behavior.

Flach, Andrew, Publisher. Thank You: 101 Ways to Practice Effortless Gratitude. USA: Hatherleigh Press, 2012.

Gilbert, Daniel. Stumbling on Happiness. New York: Vintage Books, 2007.

Hawkeye, Timber. Buddhist Boot Camp. New York: HarperOne, 2013.

Helliwell, John F., Layard Richard, and Sachs, Jeffrey D. (2018). World Happiness Report 2018, New York: Sustainable Development Solutions Network.

James, William. Pragmatism and Other Writings. New York: Penguin Books, 2000.

Laird, James D., Ph.D. Feelings: The Perception of Self (Series in Affective Science). Oxford University Press, 2007.

McGraw, Phillip C., Ph.D. Self Matters: Creating Your Life From the Inside Out. New York: Free Press, 2003.

Mejia, Zameena, "Stephen Hawking's most inspirational quotes on success and happiness." cnbc.com 14 March

2018. <https://www. cnbc.com/2018/03/14/stephen-hawkings-inspirational-quotes-on-success-and-happiness.html>.

Niven, David, Ph.D., The 100 Simple Secrets of Happy People: What Scientists Have Learned and How You Can Use It. New York: HarperSan-Francisco, 2000.

Peale, Norman Vincent, Dr., The Power of Positive Thinking. New York: Prentice-Hall, Inc., 1952

Roth, J.D., "How to be happy and lead a meaningful life." Get Rich Slowly 19 April 2018 <https: //www.getrichslowly. org/how-to-be-happy/>.

Rubin, Gretchen, The Happiness Project: Or, Why I Spent a Year Trying to Sing in the Morning, Clean My Closets, Fight Right, Read Aristotle, and Generally Have More Fun. New York: Harper Paperbacks, 2015.

Langguth Ryan, Paula, Giving Thanks: The Art of Tithing. Odenton, MD: Pellingham Casper Communications, 2005.

Deschene, Lori, "40 Ways to Let Go and Feel Less Pain." tiny Buddha: simple wisdom for complex lives 04 May 2018 <https://tinybuddha.com/blog/40-ways-to-let-go-and-feel-less-pain/>.

Seligman, Martin E.P., "Learned Optimism: How to Change Your Mind and Your Life," p.30, Vintage

Seppälä, Emma, PH.D., The Happiness Track: How to Apply the Science of Happiness to Accelerate Your Success. New York, NY: Harper Collins, 2016

Sheldon, Kennon M.; Lyubomirsky, Sonja, "Achieving Sustainable Gains in Happiness; Change Your Actions, not Your Circumstances." Journal of Happiness Studies. 2006: 7: 55-86. DOI 10.1007/s10902-005-0868-8.

Sifferlin, Alexandra, "Here's How Happy Americans Are Right Now." 07 July 2017 <http://time.com/4871720/how-happy-are-americans/>.

Stanislavski, Constantin. An Actor Prepares. New York, NY: Routledge, 1989.

Sternberg, Adam. "The Cure for New York Face. The most talked-about course in America isn't about making money or saving the world. It's about how to be really, truly happy. Here's the cheat sheet." New York Magazine 28 May 2018: 22-29

Stillman, Jessica, "Gratitude Physically Changes Your Brain, New Study Says." Inc.com 15 January 2016. <https://www.inc.com/jessica-stillman/the-amazing-way-gratitude-rewires-your-brain-for-happiness.html>.

Strauss Cohen, Ilene, Ph.D. "Important Tips on How to Let Go and Free Yourself: Twelve tips on how to let go so you can have personal freedom." Psychology Today 07 August 2017

Tadwalkar, Ruchar, "21 Signs Your Meditation & Yoga Practices Are Working." Mindbodygreen. https://www.happiness.com/en/magazine/science-psychology/proven-benefits-of-meditation/

Vilhauer, Jennice, Ph.D., "What You Can Do When You Can't Stop Thinking About Something." Psychology Today 30 December 2015<https://www.psychologytoday.com/us/blog/living-forward/201512/what-you-can-do-when-you-can't-stop-thinking-about something>

Weil, Elizabeth, "Happiness, Inc." The New York Times April 19, 2013: Fashion & Style

Wiseman, Richard. 59 Seconds: Change Your Life in Under a Minute. New York: Anchor Books, 2011.

Wolfers, Justin, "Winning the Lottery Beats Losing, a Study Finds," *The New York Times* August 26, 2018: Economic View

ABOUT THE AUTHOR

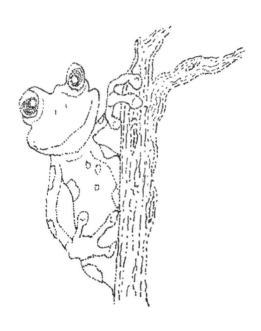

E ric J. Raff is a Human Resources professional who has led talent development for world-class ad agencies and marketing service providers. Over the years, he has coached and counseled senior managers, employees, and job candidates across all walks of life, from career development to personal life advice. He earned a BA in Psychology and an MBA in Marketing at the University of Florida and is currently the Human Resources Officer for the Art Students League of New York.

A student of psychology, management, and personal growth and development, Eric is an avid traveler who developed his personal life philosophy in the corporate world and the world at large, learning from and adding to his knowledge of human behavior from the over 70 countries and many cultures he visited during his travels around the world.

A published travel writer, songwriter, and photographer, he is the author of *No Sense of Direction*, a travelogue that described his year-long travels across Eastern Europe and Southeast Asia. He lives in New York City with his wife, Mari.

ACKNOWLEDGMENTS

A BIG thank you to my family—my mother Jean, brother Barry, sister Robin, and godson Josh, for their valuable comments, suggestions, and support in the writing of *GLAD*.

I would also like to thank my good friends Scott Soodek, Ron Pisaturo, and Karin Silbert for their helpful feedback and recommendations.

And of course, a *very special thank you* to my wife, Mari, for her ongoing support, unconditional love, and insightful illustration suggestions.

Made in the USA
Middletown, DE
19 January 2019